A Note to Parents and Teachers

DK READERS is a compelling reading programme for children, designed in conjunction with leading literacy experts, including Cliff Moon M.Ed., Honorary Fellow of the University of Reading. Cliff Moon has spent many years as a teacher and teacher educator specializing in reading and has written more than 160 books for children and teachers. He is series editor to Collins Big Cat.

Beautiful illustrations and superb full-colour photographs combine with engaging, easy-to-read stories to offer a fresh approach to each subject in the series. Each DK READER is guaranteed to capture a child's interest while developing his or her reading skills, general knowledge, and love of reading.

The five levels of DK READERS are aimed at different reading abilities, enabling you to choose the books that are exactly right for your child:

Pre-level 1: Learning to read
Level 1: Beginning to read
Level 2: Beginning to read alone
Level 3: Reading alone
Level 4: Proficient readers

The "normal" age at which a child begins to read can be anywhere from three to eight years old. Adult participation through the lower levels is very helpful for providing encouragement, discussing storylines and sounding out unfamiliar words.

No matter which level you select, you can be sure that you are helping your child learn to read, then read to learn!

D0316899

LONDON, NEW YORK, MUNICH,
MELBOURNE and DELHI

Series Editor Deborah Lock
Managing Art Editor Rachael Foster
Designer Gemma Fletcher
Production Georgina Hayworth
DTP Designer Emma Hansen
Jacket Designer Gemma Fletcher
Picture Researcher Rob Nunn

Reading Consultant
Cliff Moon, M.Ed.

Published in Great Britain by
Dorling Kindersley Limited
80 Strand, London WC2R ORL

Copyright © 2007 Dorling Kindersley Limited
A Penguin Company

2 4 6 8 10 9 7 5 3 1
RD129 - 11/06

A CIP catalogue record for this book
is available from the British Library

ISBN: 978-1-4053-1940-9

Colour reproduction by Colourscan, Singapore
Printed and bound in China by L Rex Printing Co., Ltd.

The publisher would like to thank the following for their kind
permission to reproduce their photographs:
a=above; c=centre; b=below; l=left; r=right; t=top
Alamy Images: Pegaz 17; Phototake Inc. 26; Mark Scott 18. Corbis:
Layne Kennedy 12-13 (b/g); William Whitehurst 30-31 (b/g). Getty
Images: Stone+/Siri Stafford 9. PunchStock: Digital Vision 15;
Photodisc Blue 4; Photodisc Green 19, 30l; Purestock 22; Stockbyte
11. Science Photo Library: John Sanford 29 (b/g).

All other images © Dorling Kindersley
For further information see: www.dkimages.com

Discover more at

www.dk.com

Contents

DK READERS

My
Dressing-up
Box

A Dorling Kindersley Book

4

Here is my dressing-up box. What can I be?

I can be a princess.
Here is my crown.

crown

 princess

ribbons

7

I can be a wizard.
Here is my cloak.

cloak

broom

wizard

hat

flag

pirate

I can be a pirate.
Here is my eye patch.

eye patch

shell

mermaid

I can be a mermaid.
Here is my tail.

tail

I can be a cowboy.
Here is my hat.

hat

lasso

 cowboy

I can be a fairy.
Here are my wings.

wings

fairy

dress

17

cape

superhero

I can be a superhero.
Here is my cape.

shorts

tiara

tutu

ballerina

I can be a ballerina.
Here is my tutu.

dungarees

builder

I can be a builder.
Here is my hard hat.

hard hat

I can be a firefighter.
Here is my helmet.

helmet

firefighter

hose

doctor

I can be a doctor.
Here is my sick teddy.

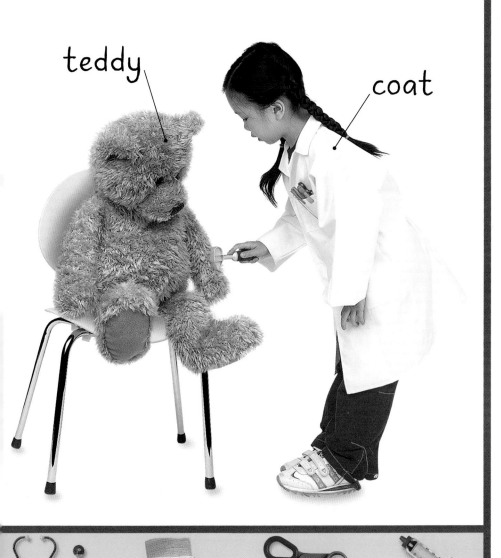

teddy

coat

I can be an astronaut.
Here is my space suit.

space suit

astronaut

We are all dressed up.
Let's put on a show!

What can you be?

Glossary

Astronaut a person who travels in space

Ballerina a woman who dances ballet

Firefighter a person who puts out fires

Mermaid a fairy-tale woman with a fish tail instead of legs

Princess the daughter of a king and queen